Name: Denis Bouzon

Date of Birth: 04/16/97

Classroom #: 309

Date of Donation: 04/06

MOUNTAINS

The Tops of the World

by **David L. Harrison**

Illustrated by **Cheryl Nathan**

Boyds Mills Press

The author wishes to thank Erwin J. Mantei, Ph.D., Professor of
Geology, Southwest Missouri State University, for his review of the
text and illustrations.

Published by Boyds Mills Press, Inc.
A Highlights Company
815 Church Street
Honesdale, Pennsylvania 18431
Printed in China

Library of Congress Cataloging-in-Publication Data

Harrison, David L.
Mountains : the tops of the world / by David L. Harrison ; illustrated by Cheryl Nathan.— 1st ed.
p. cm. — (Earthworks)
ISBN 1-59078-326-3 (alk. paper)
1. Mountains—Juvenile literature. I. Nathan, Cheryl, 1958- ill. II. Title. III. Series: Earthworks (Honesdale, Pa.)

GB512.H37 2005
551.43—dc22

2004029067

First edition, 2005
The text is set in 14-point Optima.
The illustrations are done digitally.

Visit our Web site at www.boydsmillspress.com

10 9 8 7 6 5 4 3 2 1

To Larry Rosler, my editor and collaborator for Earthworks
—D. L. H.

For Ralph and Helen Nathan
—C. N.

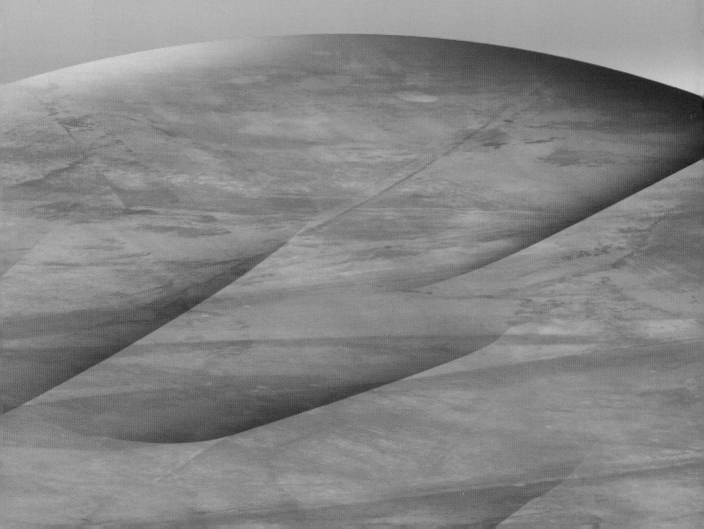

Here is how a fish from the sea
could reach the top of a mountain:
The fish dies and sinks to the bottom.
Sand hides the body
from hungry creatures.
For millions of years,
more sand settles across the sea floor.
Tiny dead plants and creatures
seep down through the water.
These layers of sand and debris
are called sediments.

The weight of sediments on top
squeezes the water from layers below
and presses those sediments together
into sedimentary rock.
The fish turns to stone, too,
and becomes a fossil.
The fossil fish might lie
forever buried beneath the sea,
but tectonic plates will move it.

Tectonic plates
are slabs of rock so big
they carry oceans and continents
on their backs.
Together they form
Earth's outer crust.
Below the plates lies the mantle.
Rock there is so hot it melts
and flows in slow currents
that move the plates like rafts.

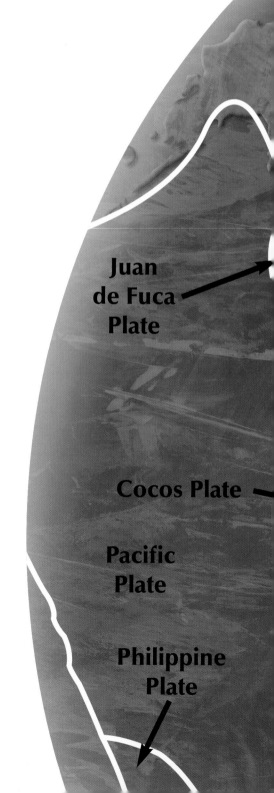

Juan de Fuca Plate

Cocos Plate

Pacific Plate

Philippine Plate

Plates creep slower than hair grows.
Some of them rub past each other.
When their jagged edges catch and snap,
the jolts cause earthquakes.
Some plates collide,
and one is forced under the other.

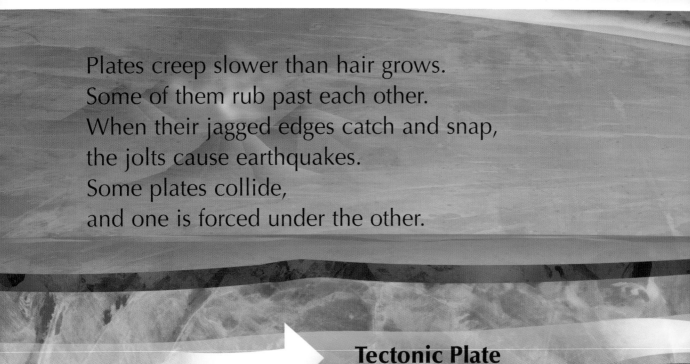

Tectonic Plate

The bottom edge slides into the mantle,
where it melts and is called magma.
Magma and hot ashes
escaping through the crust
may cool and build up mountains
called volcanoes.

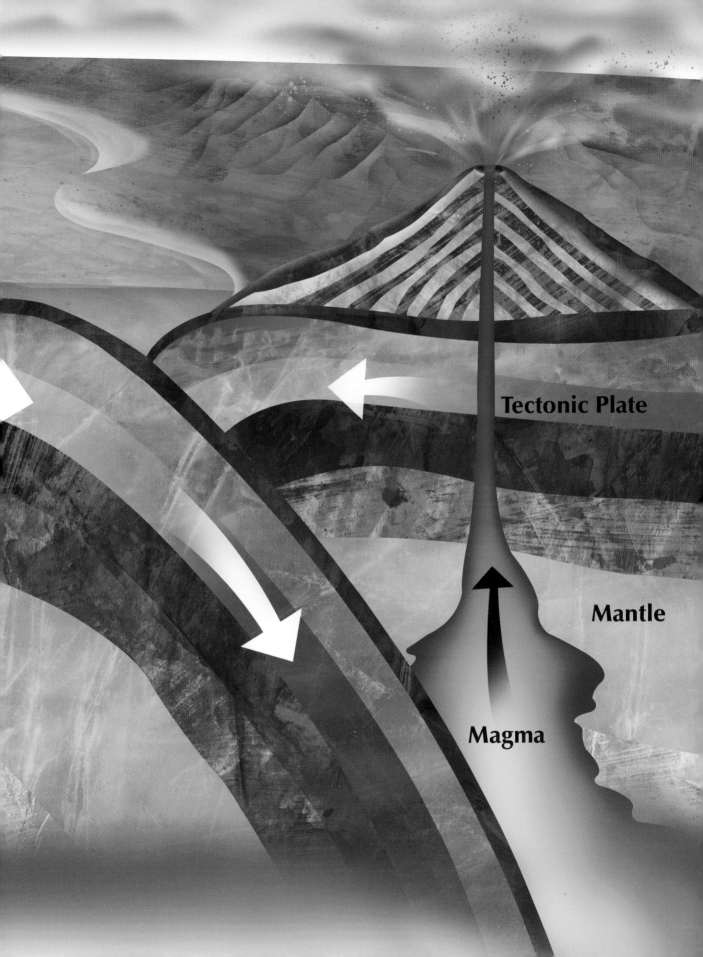

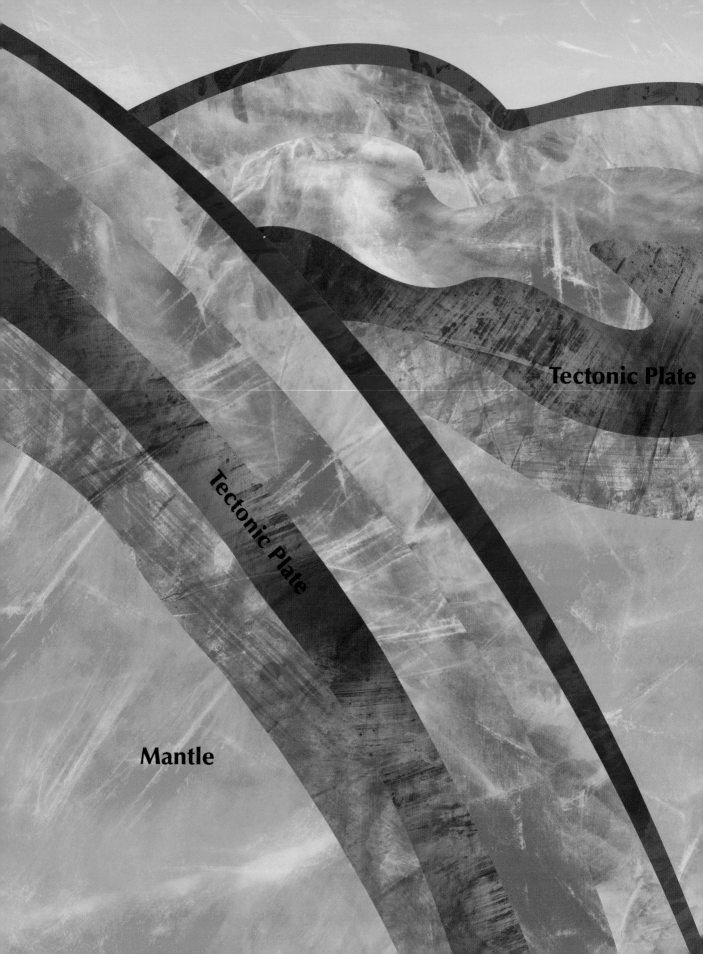

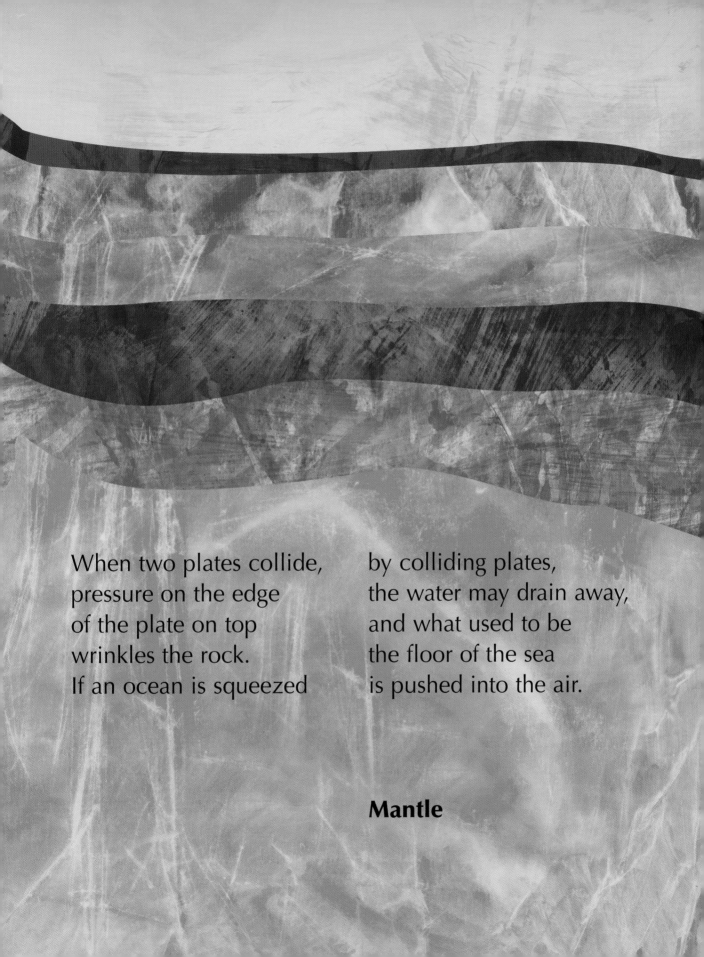

When two plates collide,
pressure on the edge
of the plate on top
wrinkles the rock.
If an ocean is squeezed

by colliding plates,
the water may drain away,
and what used to be
the floor of the sea
is pushed into the air.

Mantle

As the wrinkles
  on the plate on top grow,
    layers of rock bend and fold
      higher and higher.
        Mount Everest began as a wrinkle
        when the plate that carries India
          rammed the plate that carries Asia
          about fifty million years ago.
          It is now the world's tallest peak —
          29,000 feet high —
              higher than many airplanes fly.

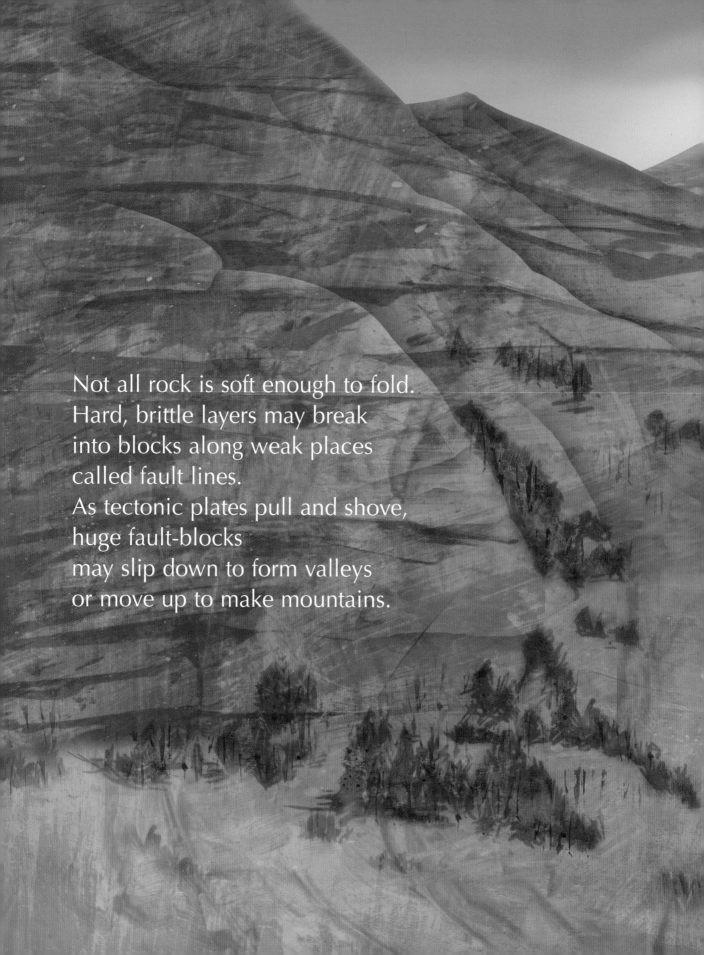

Not all rock is soft enough to fold.
Hard, brittle layers may break
into blocks along weak places
called fault lines.
As tectonic plates pull and shove,
huge fault-blocks
may slip down to form valleys
or move up to make mountains.

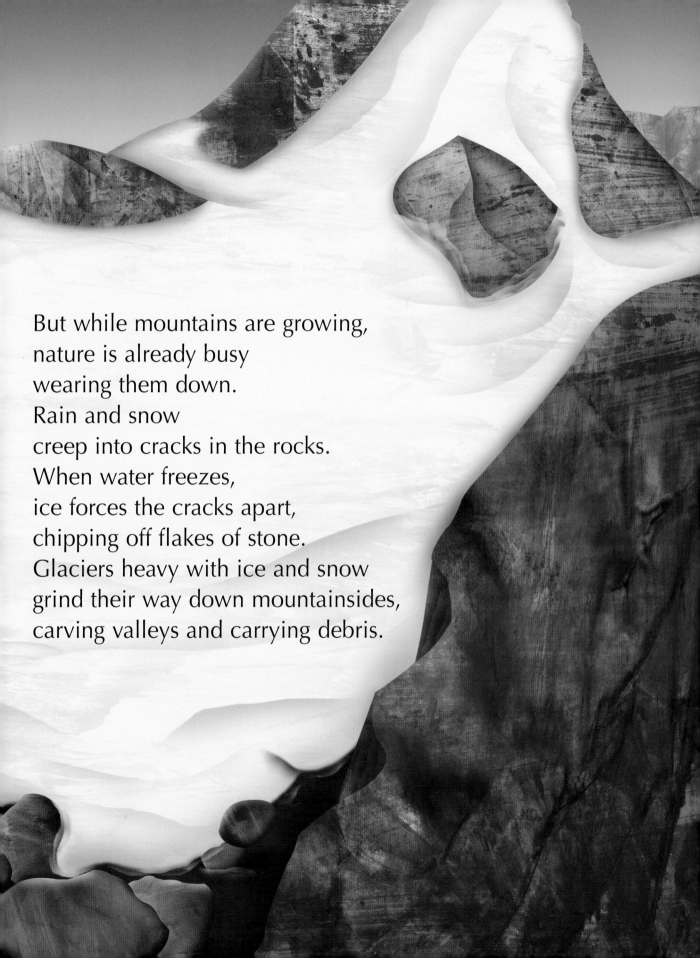

But while mountains are growing,
nature is already busy
wearing them down.
Rain and snow
creep into cracks in the rocks.
When water freezes,
ice forces the cracks apart,
chipping off flakes of stone.
Glaciers heavy with ice and snow
grind their way down mountainsides,
carving valleys and carrying debris.

On lower slopes,
roots of trees
and other plants
pry into cracks,
making more chips fall.

Waterfalls and rivers
tumbling down valleys
send the chips
on a long journey
toward the sea.

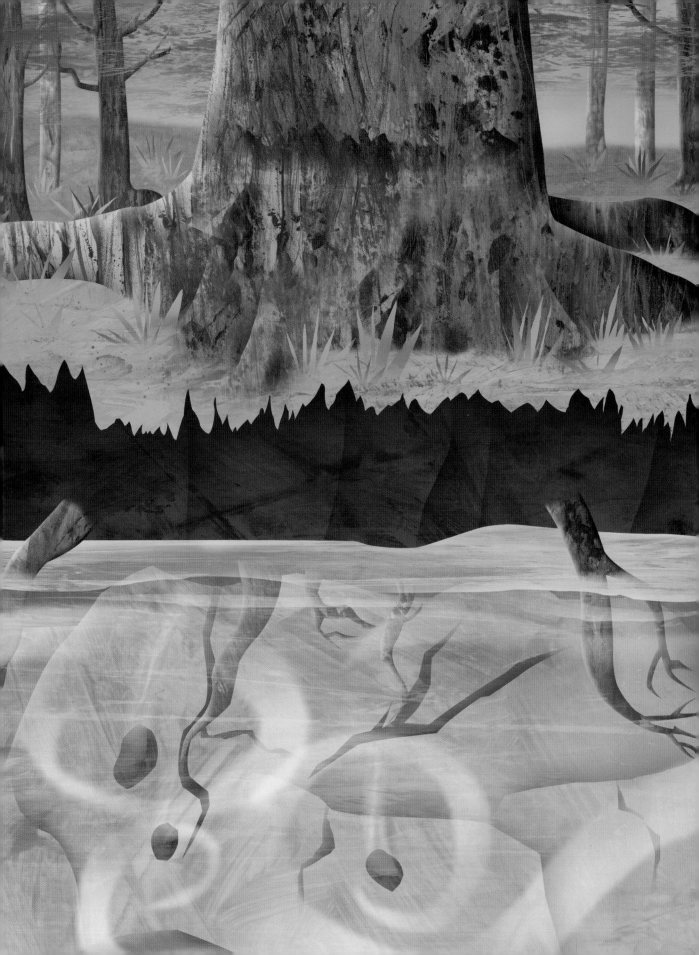

Little by little,
mountains wear down
like ice-cream sundaes
melting and shrinking.
Over millions of years,
their peaks grow rounder.
Their frosty caps
of ice and snow are
replaced by sturdy forests.
More and more animals make
the mountains their home.
People hike along their trails,
fish in their streams,
and camp in their woods.

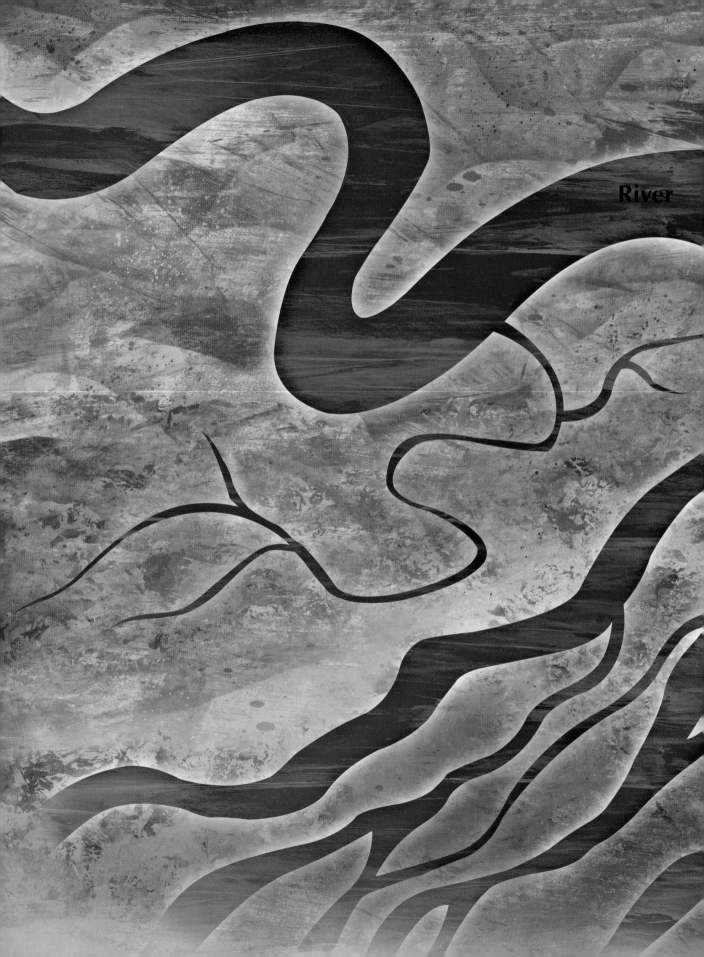

River

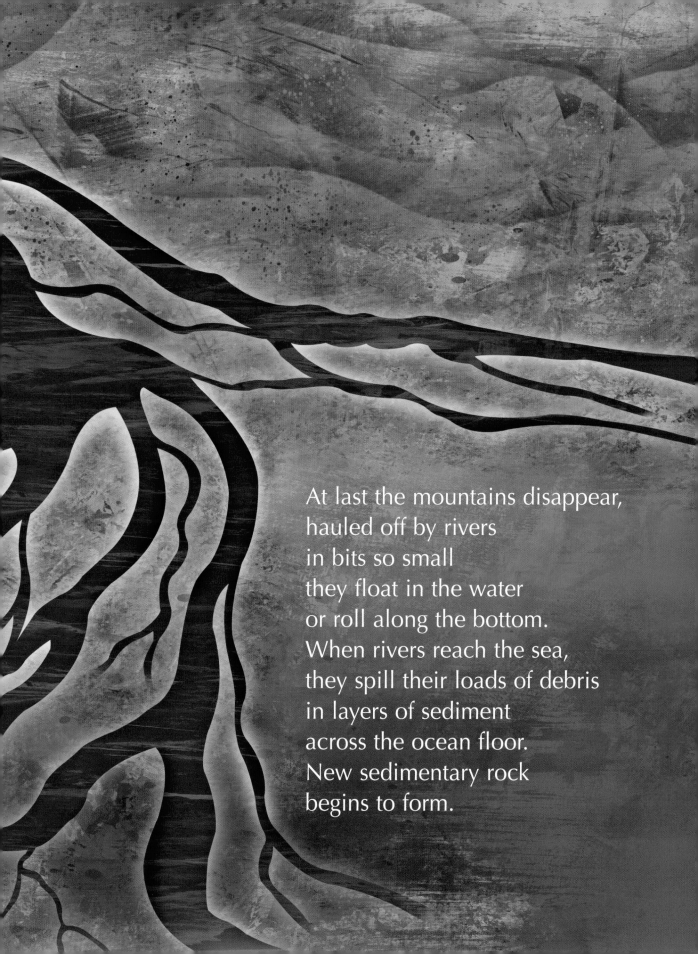

At last the mountains disappear,
hauled off by rivers
in bits so small
they float in the water
or roll along the bottom.
When rivers reach the sea,
they spill their loads of debris
in layers of sediment
across the ocean floor.
New sedimentary rock
begins to form.

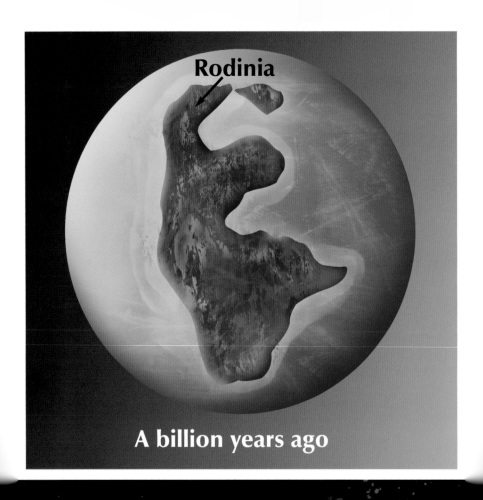

A billion years ago

Earth never stops changing.
A billion years or so ago,
all the land was clustered
into one continent
around the South Pole.
Scientists call it Rodinia (ro-DIN-ee-a).
Hundreds of millions of years later,
Rodinia broke apart.
A sea called Lapetus (LAP-i-tus) separated
North America and Europe
the way the Atlantic Ocean does today

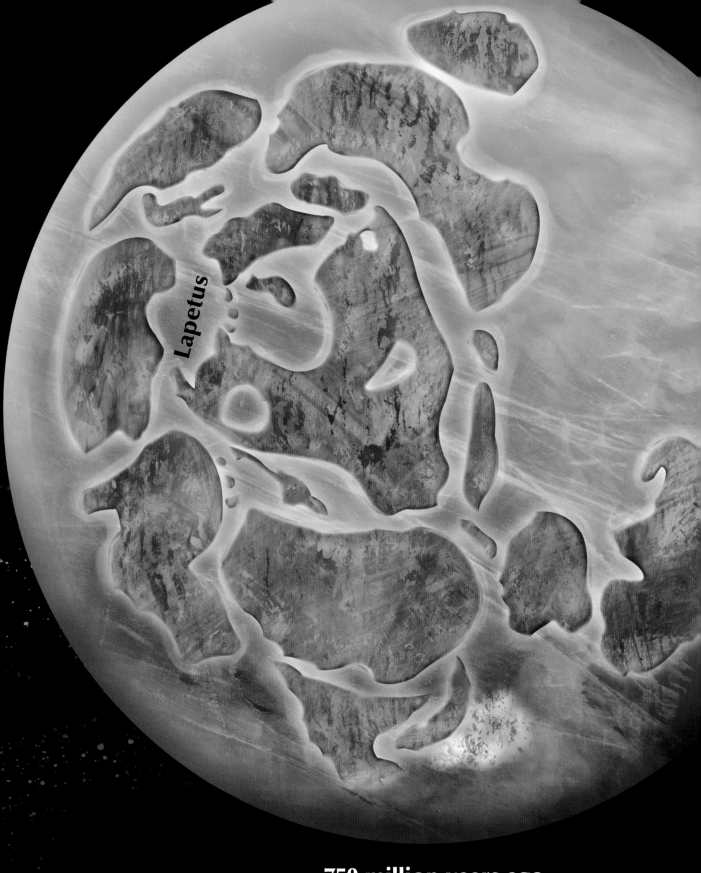

Iapetus

750 million years ago

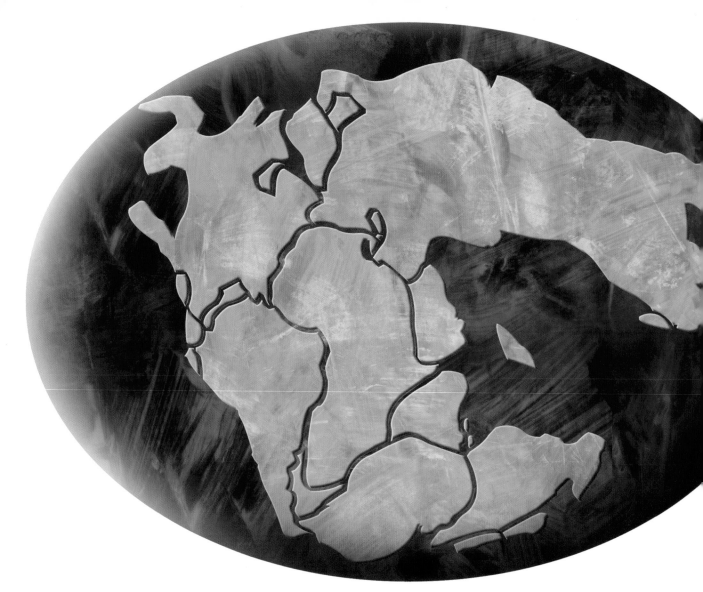

Pangaea

Many millions of years later,
the lands came back together,
squeezing out Lapetus
to form a single continent.
Scientists call this continent Pangaea (pan-GEE-uh).

Later, Pangaea also broke apart,
and the world began to look
the way it does today.
Lapetus is gone,
replaced by the Atlantic Ocean,
which is still growing.

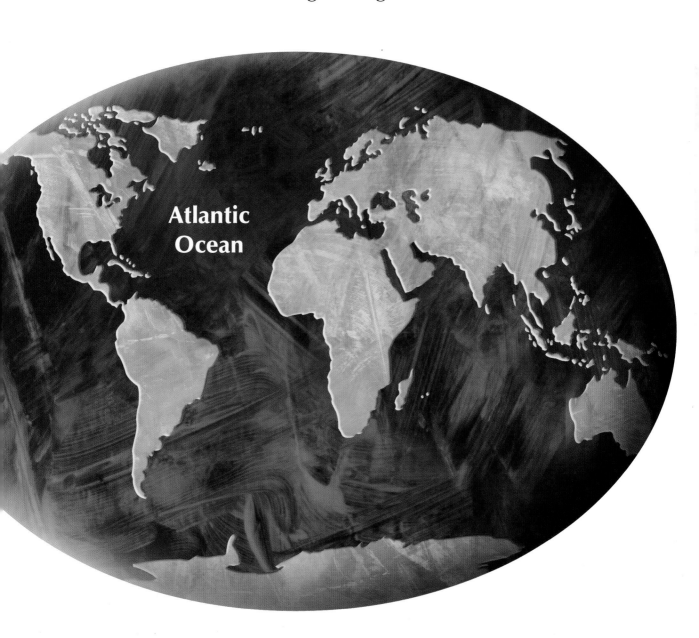

Atlantic
Ocean

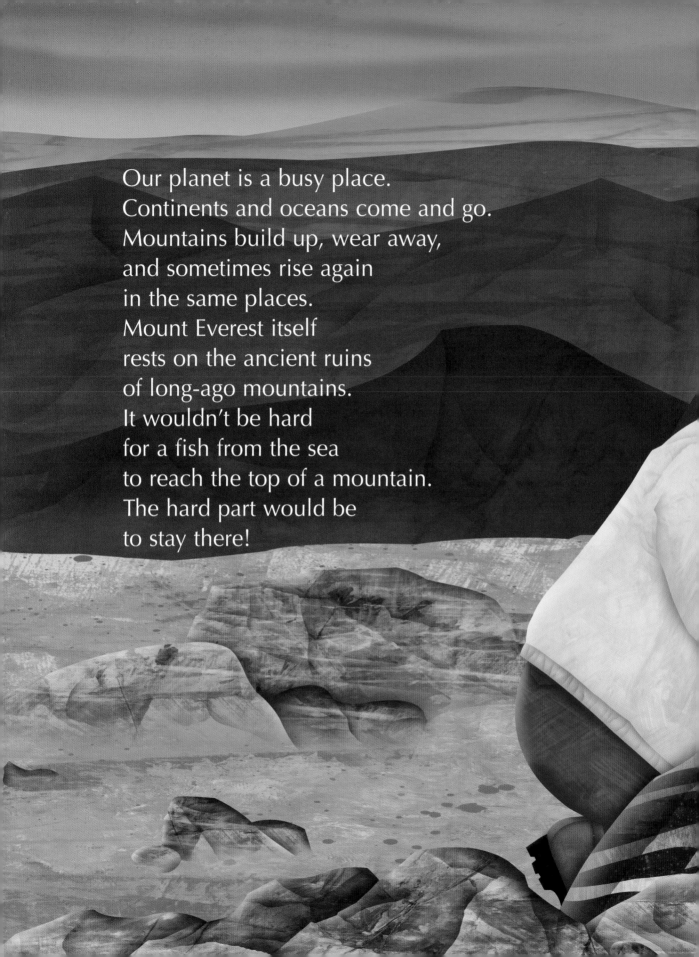

Our planet is a busy place.
Continents and oceans come and go.
Mountains build up, wear away,
and sometimes rise again
in the same places.
Mount Everest itself
rests on the ancient ruins
of long-ago mountains.
It wouldn't be hard
for a fish from the sea
to reach the top of a mountain.
The hard part would be
to stay there!

AUTHOR'S NOTE

For as long as people have walked on Earth, we've looked to mountains as symbols of strength and endurance. Nothing seems bigger or more permanent. Yet even mountains must submit to superior strength. Whether forged by the fires of volcanic magma or thrust toward the sky by tectonic plates, mountains are no match for the patient, unrelenting forces that eventually wear them away.

Paint peeling from houses and chips flaking off bricks demonstrate what nature can do in even a few years. But building a mountain and then tearing it down requires a scale of time that is hard to imagine. Throughout its 4.6 billion years, Earth has never stopped fiddling with its face. Tectonic plates shove continents around as if they are rearranging furniture. Approximately 200 million years ago, the plates that brought together all the land to form Pangaea began crawling off again in different directions. From that time, the Atlantic Ocean has expanded by about one inch per year. Today it measures 3,000 miles across. Since Columbus sailed the ocean in 1492, the Atlantic has added a little more than 40 feet.

The Atlantic has spread 60 miles or so since some of mankind's earliest ancestors walked in the open woodlands of Kenya 4 million years ago. By then India's Himalayan Mountains had been forming for at least 36 million years. North America's Appalachian Mountains had probably celebrated their 200-millionth anniversary. Piecing together puzzles that take so long to complete is the job of geologists who study orogeny (mountain building). They have learned much about the rhythms and patterns of nature. We know now that change on Earth is inevitable. The idea that mountains don't last forever makes them more interesting and precious. In this basic introduction, I've tried to convey that mountains make a fascinating subject. Here are some other books for young readers recommended by librarians.

— **David L. Harrison**

FURTHER READING

Ganeri, Anita. *Mountains*. Milwaukee: Gareth Stevens Publishing, 2003.
Stronach, Neil. *Mountains*. Minneapolis: Lerner Publications Co., 1996.
Baker, Susan. *Mountains*. Milwaukee: Gareth Stevens Children's Books, 1991.
Jennings, Terry. *Mountains*. Mankato, Minnesota: Thameside Press, 2002.
Taylor, Barbara. *Mountains and Volcanoes*. Boston: Houghton Mifflin, 2002.
Robson, Pam. *Mountains and Our Moving Earth*. Brookfield, Connecticut: Copper Beech Books, 2001.